DEVELOPING POSITIVE ASSERTIVENESS

Revised Edition

Sam R. Lloyd

A FIFTY-MINUTE™ SERIES BOOK

CRISP PUBLICATIONS, INC.
Menlo Park, California

DEVELOPING POSITIVE ASSERTIVENESS
Revised Edition

Sam R. Lloyd

CREDITS
Editor: **Michael Crisp**
Typesetting: **ExecuStaff**
Cover Design: **Carol Harris**
Artwork: **Ralph Mapson**

Copyright © 1988, 1995 by Crisp Publications, Inc.

Printed in the United States of America by Bawden Printing Company.

Distribution to the U.S. Trade:

National Book Network, Inc.
4720 Boston Way
Lanham, MD 20706
1-800-462-6420

Library of Congress Catalog Card Number 94-72612
Lloyd, Sam R.
Developing Positive Assertiveness
ISBN 1-56052-313-1

This book is printed on recyclable paper with soy ink.

ABOUT THIS BOOK

Developing Positive Assertiveness is not like most books. It stands out from other self-help books in an important way. It's not a book to read, it's a book to *use*. The unique "self-paced" format of this book encourages a reader to get involved and try some new ideas immediately.

This book will provide an awareness and understanding of what assertive behavior is and why it is desirable and important for you to develop and use assertive behavior in your natural style. Using the simple yet sound techniques presented can help any reader learn to become more assertive.

Developing Positive Assertiveness can be used effectively in a number of ways. Here are some possibilities:

—**Self Study.** Because the book is self-instructional, all that is needed is a quiet place, and some time. By completing the activities and exercises, a reader should receive valuable ideas about how to become more assertive.

—**Workshops and Seminars.** The book is ideal for assigned reading prior to a workshop or seminar. With the basics in hand, the quality of the participation will improve, and more time can be spent on concept extensions and applications during the program. The book is also effective when it is distributed at the beginning of a session, and participants "work through" the contents.

—**Remote Location Training.** Books can be sent to those not able to attend "home office" training sessions.

There are several other possibilities that depend on the objectives, program or ideas of the user.

One thing for sure, even after it has been read, this book will be looked at—and thought about—again and again.

ABOUT THE AUTHOR

Sam R. Lloyd is President of SuccessSystems, Inc., of Dallas, Texas. He is a past Director of the Management Center of Southern Methodist University and has also been Assistant Dean of the School of Business at University of Missouri, St. Louis.

For the past ten years, Mr. Lloyd has trained thousands of individuals in many major organizations, including Monsanto, E.I. DuPont, IBM, General Telephone and General Foods among others.

He specializes in Assertiveness Training, Listening Skills, Interpersonal Effectiveness, Negotiation and Customer Relations.

Mr. Lloyd is a member of ITAA, ASTD and is listed in *Who's Who.*

PREFACE

This book is for anyone who wants to take charge and live life. Developing positive assertiveness can mean the difference in creating personal success and making things happen for you.

Will reading this book result in your being assertive? Not if all you do is read. If however, you read and complete the exercises and practice the techniques as recommended, you will learn how to develop positive assertiveness. The book can't make you assertive, but you can!

Developing assertiveness is more that just learning to talk differently. Being assertive requires THINKING assertively, FEELING confident and BEHAVING positively. In this book you will learn how to develop each of these aspects of assertiveness. Explanations of personality and psychological concepts will help you understand about yourself and other people. Guidelines for word choices and behaviors will help you change how you interact with others. Several exercises will help you change your attitudes that interfere with being assertive.

Assertive people enjoy their work, play, friends and family. Assertive people are effective, vital and valued by others. With this book, some personal commitment and a little time, you can become an assertive person and experience these benefits for the rest of your life!

You Can Do It!

Sam R. Lloyd

CONTENTS

CONTENTS (continued)

INTRODUCTION

Assertive Behavior and Why It Is Important

What do you think of when you hear the word "Assertive"? Many people think of someone adamantly standing their ground, pushing for his or her own way, refusing to give an inch. Others think of someone who is generally pleasant but stubborn on certain issues. Most people don't understand what "Assertive Behavior" really is.

Assertive behavior as defined in this book is a natural style that is nothing more than being direct, honest and respectful while interacting with others. So what's the big deal? Why is there a need for assertiveness training courses and books? Why do cartoonists poke fun at assertiveness training? Why does management in some organizations resist when assertiveness training is mentioned?

The poking fun and open resistance are symptoms of a lack of understanding. When people do not understand, it is normal to resist change. We believe that assertiveness is the most desirable human behavior! It is needed for honest, healthy relationships. It is the behavior required for "win-win" outcomes in negotiation, conflict resolution, family life and normal business dealings.

The courses, books and cassette tapes are necessary because so many people do not understand the desirability and importance of using assertive behavior. As more people develop assertiveness and influence others, the awareness and acceptance of assertiveness will increase. This book explains why people have to make a conscious effort to develop their assertiveness. Even though assertive behavior *is* natural, it is not the only natural behavior! We humans also use nonassertive and aggressive behavior. These styles create many problems in our relationships, business dealings and social interactions.

All of us use all three behavior styles throughout our lives. Most of us are not as consistently assertive as we might think. When we learn to become more assertive we can reduce our conflicts, failures, dissatisfactions and stresses. Developing assertiveness requires effort, but the rewards are worth it. This book will provide you with information, simple directions and plenty of opportunities to practice becoming more assertive.

INTRODUCTION (continued)

After first finding out how assertive you are right now, you will then learn how to identify the three behavior styles previously mentioned (assertive, nonassertive and aggressive). You will also learn how to assure successful change, and how to develop positive assertiveness. Once you have learned to develop your assertiveness, you will finally learn how to maintain the changes you have made. All of this in less than 100 pages. Whew!

The first step is to find out how assertive you are now.

AN ASSERTIVENESS QUIZ

Before learning how to develop your assertiveness, it is important to take a few moments to get some idea of where you are right now. Answer the questions below honestly. They will help you gain some insights about your current level of assertiveness.

Assign a number to each item using this scale:

ALWAYS				NEVER
5	4	3	2	1

_____ I ask others to do things without feeling guilty or anxious.

_____ When someone asks me to do something I don't want to do, I say "no" without feeling guilty or anxious.

_____ I am comfortable when speaking to a large group of people.

_____ I confidently express my honest opinions to authority figures (such as my boss).

_____ When I experience powerful feelings (anger, frustration, disappointment, etc.), I verbalize them easily.

_____ When I express anger, I do so without blaming others for "making me mad."

_____ I am comfortable speaking up in a group situation.

_____ If I disagree with the majority opinion in a meeting, I can "stick to my guns" without feeling uncomfortable or being abrasive.

_____ When I make a mistake, I will acknowledge it.

_____ I tell others when their behavior creates a problem for me.

_____ Meeting new people in social situations is something I do with ease and comfort.

_____ When discussing my beliefs, I do so without labeling the opinions of others as "crazy," "stupid," "ridiculous," "irrational."

AN ASSERTIVENESS QUIZ (continued)

_____ I assume that most people are competent and trustworthy and do not have difficulty delegating tasks to others.

_____ When considering doing something I have never done, I feel confident I can learn to do it.

_____ I believe my needs are as important as those of others and I am entitled to have my needs satisfied.

> Total Score (Sum of the 15 numbers)
>
> Turn the page to learn your present level of assertiveness.

HOW ASSERTIVE ARE YOU?

If your total is 60 or higher, you have a consistently assertive philosophy and probably handle most situations well. You may receive some ideas from this book to further improve your skills and effectiveness.

If your total is 45-60, you have a fairly assertive outlook. There are some situations in which you may be naturally assertive, but the book will help you to increase your assertiveness through practice.

If your total is 30-45, you seem to be assertive in some situations but your natural response is either nonassertive or aggressive. Using the suggestions in this book to change some perceptions and practicing new behaviors should allow you to handle things much more assertively in the future.

If your total is 15-30, you have considerable difficulty being assertive. If you follow the road outlined in this book, practice and allow yourself time to grow and change, you can become much more comfortable in situations where asserting yourself is important.

P A R T

I

How to Develop Positive Assertiveness

You
and
Positive
Assertiveness

THREE BASIC BEHAVIOR STYLES

It would be nice if you could simply decide to go down the road marked "Assertive" and live your life without straying from the path.

Real life is full of twists and turns and no one is consistently assertive. All of us use the three basic behavior styles described below depending on the situation and personal factors. The good news is that we can learn to become more assertive more of the time.

1. **NONASSERTIVE** behavior is passive and indirect. It communicates a message of inferiority. By being nonassertive we allow the wants, needs and rights of others to be more important than our own. Nonassertive behavior helps create "win-lose" situations. A person behaving nonassertively will lose (or at best be disregarded) while allowing others to win. Following this road leads to being a victim, not a winner.

2. **AGGRESSIVE** behavior is more complex. It can be either active or passive. Aggression can be direct or indirect, honest or dishonest—but it always communicates an impression of superiority and disrespect. By being aggressive we put our wants, needs and rights above those of others. We attempt to get our way by not allowing others a choice. Aggressive behavior is usually inappropriate because it violates the rights of others. People behaving aggressively may "win" by making sure others "lose"—but in doing so set themselves up for retaliation. No one likes a bully.

3. **ASSERTIVE** behavior is active, direct and honest. It communicates an impression of self-respect and respect for others. By being assertive we view our wants, needs and rights as equal with those of others. We work toward "win-win" outcomes. An assertive person wins by influencing, listening and negotiating so that others choose to cooperate willingly. This behavior leads to success without retaliation and encourages open, honest relationships!

BEHAVIOR STYLES QUIZ

Identify each behavior style in the following examples and write you answer in the space.

Using the abbreviations: NAS=Nonassertive AS=Assertive AG=Aggressive, then check your answers with those of the author.

_____ **1.** "Only an idiot would think of a solution like that! Don't you ever think before you talk?"

_____ **2.** "You know, maybe we might want to think about a different alternative, uh, what do you think?"

_____ **3.** "Oh, I can't go—I have other plans."

_____ **4.** "I'm not completely comfortable with your solution. Will you please develop at least one more option?"

_____ **5.** "No, thank you. I appreciate your asking, but I really don't enjoy opera."

_____ **6.** "Opera! You've got to be kidding!"

_____ **7.** "This probably isn't what you wanted, but I guess I wasn't too sure about what you said, and, anyway, I'm not very good at this kind of thing."

_____ **8.** "Well, okay, if that's what you want to do."

_____ **9.** "Great idea! Let's do it!"

_____ **10.** "Tracy, please send this to all regional offices today."

Compare your answers with the author's on the facing page.

Author's Answers

1. AG—Accusatory, exaggerated, blameful, invites defensiveness.

2. NAS—Hesitant, passive, apologetic, invites disregard.

3. NAS—Plans are only plans and can be changed. This is a subtle dishonesty and is one of the most common ways of avoiding having to say "no."

4. AS—Honest, respectful, invites cooperation.

5. AS—Honest, tactful, firm but appreciative (compare to #3).

6. AG—Sarcastic, blameful, invites defensiveness.

7. NAS—Self-deprecating, defensive, invites disrespect.

8. NAS—Hesitant, deferential, possibly dishonest about wants.

9. AS—Enthusiastic, genuine, cooperative.

10. AS—Direct, respectful, invites cooperation.

CAN BEHAVIORS CHANGE?

Do you believe you can't change your basic personality? If so, you and the experts agree. Most experts concur that a general "personality type" cannot be changed. Once you have developed your basic personality (between ages 5 and 12), your most natural psychological characteristics do not really change much.

If this is the case, you might ask, "Is it a waste of time to engage in self-improvement?" The answer is NO! Even if your core characteristics are permanent, it is possible to change many things about yourself. Things you can change include your beliefs, attitudes, goals, expectations, word choices and body language to mention a few. Modestly changing any of these factors can result in your being assertive more often. When this happens, you win!

Before we figure out which direction you need to travel, it will be helpful if you understand your starting point. Answer the items on the next page (as honestly as you can) to gain a better awareness of your personality characteristics. Your natural response will provide the most accurate insights.

A PERSONALITY QUIZ

Answer the following questions honestly and then check the next page for your starting point.

TRUE or FALSE

_____ 1. I almost always speak or make eye contact first when encountering another person.

_____ 2. I prefer being with several people rather than having a one-on-one conversation in social situations.

_____ 3. I prefer to eat lunch alone.

_____ 4. The best way to make a decision is to assemble all of the facts first.

_____ 5. When I want to have fun, I do something exciting, something with lots of action.

_____ 6. The most important thing in life is having good relationships with family and friends.

_____ 7. When I go to meetings or parties, I spend most of the time talking with one person at a time rather that interacting with a group.

_____ 8. The best way to learn something is to jump in and do it.

_____ 9. I am very aware of how others respond to me and often worry about whether they like me or if I have displeased them.

_____ 10. When I make a decision I trust my intuition—somehow I seem to sense what is best.

_____ 11. I am usually the one to initiate things, either social activities or business.

_____ 12. Spending an evening discussing current events, work-related topics, or philosophical issues can be very stimulating and interesting.

_____ 13. When I am with others we usually discuss relationships, personal difficulties or how we feel about our lives.

_____ 14. My favorite topic is what people have done, where they have been and what happened. I enjoy telling others about my adventures.

PERSONALITY QUIZ (continued)

Author's Answers

If you answered 1, 4, 7, 11 and 12 true and the others false, you are an active initiator who prefers one-on-one interaction. You seem to be a THINKER who plans and you are careful and methodical.

If you answered 2, 6, 9, 10, 11 and 13 true and most others false, you seem to be an active initiator who is social and caring. You are a FEELER in touch with your emotions. You value personal relationships and want to please people.

If you answered 5, 8, 10 and 14 true and most others false, you are more passive than initiative with people. You are less involved with people and more interested in physical activities. You are a DOER who enjoys the pleasure of being active. You are not likely to be comfortable around others when they discuss feelings.

What about Question 3? If you like to eat lunch alone, this indicates you need solitude. THINKERS and some DOERS often are more withdrawing than involving. This means they are comfortable being alone. Most FEELERS, many THINKERS and some DOERS have a greater need to be with people.

There are many other psychological groupings. There are also more sophisticated questionnaires which identify these groups. In this book, we have tried to keep things simple and limited ourselves to three general groupings; THINKERS, FEELERS and DOERS. These three are sufficient to provide insight into some of the most basic *automatic* behaviors and orientations toward life. Awareness of which group you are in should help you understand why you are more comfortable in certain situations than others. It also helps explain why others often approach life differently than you do.

Each personality type is OK! It is natural to consider the group we identify with as somehow "better" than the others. One type however, is no better than another; it is simply different. All types are essential and all contribute to life, organizations and families. Each has different strengths and each approaches work and life differently. Accepting this reality is an important step to develop an *assertive,* win-win approach with others.

A PEOPLE-WATCHING EXERCISE

At a professional conference the following people were observed at the social "mixer" held at the conclusion of the first day. John arrived exactly at the time listed for the "mixer," paused at the entrance of the room to survey the crowd and purposefully walked to the refreshment area to obtain a drink. After getting his drink, he looked around again and saw someone he knew. Approaching his acquaintance, he made eye contact and spoke, "Hi, Mary. Have you been here long?" They talked for some time and the man returned to the refreshment area while looking around the room again. Which type is John?

Martha arrived after John. She entered the room and immediately walked toward a group of four people who were near. She introduced herself, "Hi everybody, I'm Martha and I'm really enjoying this conference. Are you?" She quickly met everyone and joined in their conversation about the day. Soon the group was sharing information about their families. Martha noticed a friend arrive, waved with a big smile, and motioned her friend to come join the group. Which type is Martha?

Sometime later Paula arrived. She had been returning some telephone calls and completing an analysis of a colleague's proposal as she had promised she would do. When Paula arrived she paused at the door to see if she recognized anyone. Seeing someone she knew, Paula walked over and the pair spent the entire time in an involved conversation about the problems of world peace. Which type is Paula?

Right after Paula entered the room, Bob arrived. He burst into the room, rushed to the refreshment area for a drink, spotted some people he had seen earlier and walked over to them. Someone looked up at him and Bob said, "Hey! Where's the party? Nothing's happening—let's get something going here!" Within a few minutes the group left the "mixer" to go to an area of town where Bob had learned that live entertainment was available.

After finding the area, the group went to a building which housed several night clubs that offered dancing. Bob turned out to be an expert dancer and spent the evening dancing with various members of the group. Which type is Bob?

See Next Page For Answers

A PEOPLE-WATCHING EXERCISE (continued)

Author's Answers

Easy, isn't it? John was a THINKER, Martha was a FEELER, Paula was another THINKER and Bob was a DOER. All four are successful individuals and lead happy, meaningful lives. They all have different styles and react differently to situations.

To one degree or another, all personality types use all three behavior styles. With better awareness and practice, it is possible to increase assertiveness and decrease nonassertive and aggressive choices. Simply stated, all of us can learn to change.

PART

II

Assuring Successful Change

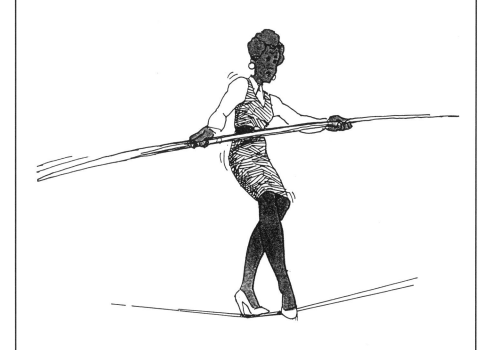

THE FIVE Ps OF SUCCESSFUL CHANGE

Any change, large or small, is challenging. Many psychotherapists are aware that for many people significant change usually occurs only after some traumatic experience. You don't have to wait for some traumatic event to trigger change. You do however, need to be prepared for change to make certain that change will be successful. The following guidelines will help to guarantee any successful changes you wish to make.

1. PROTECTION. Change is often scary! Have you ever made a New Year's resolution and failed to keep it? One reason we don't change, even when we truly want to, is fear. Often our fear is vague and unidentified, but it is enough to sabotage changing. *Protection* can help you stick with a commitment to change. Here are some protection suggestions:

- Start your change in your safest environment.
- Change one thing at at time—slow and easy does it.
- Whenever you feel unsure or anxious, answer these questions:
  "What's the worst that can happen?"
  "What's the probability that it will happen?"
  "What can I do to prevent it or lower the probability?"

2. POTENCY. Change is an active process, not a passive one. To activate your personal power it is necessary to invest some mental effort, emotional involvement and physical activity to changing. You can learn to tap into your potency if you:

- Define your change goal in simple, active, positive words.
- Write your change goal and post it where you see it daily.
- Imagine yourself practicing your change goal and visualize yourself doing it well.
- Tell yourself daily, "I can . . . ," "I will . . . ," and "I am . . . "

THE FIVE Ps OF SUCCESSFUL CHANGE (continued)

3. PERMISSION. Each of us requires *permission* to change. Be sure to give yourself permission and also get permission from significant others in your life who will be affected by your changes. Without their permission and support, you may not succeed.

- Tell each person what you plan to do and why.
- Ask each, "Is that O.K. with you?"

Most significant others will appreciate your consideration of their involvement with your changes. Most will say "go for it" when you ask. If someone says "no," determine the reason for the reluctance. It might be an important issue to explore and could help you redefine your change goal.

You do not need permission from everyone who is important in your life to change, but having permission from them will ease the pressure on you and normally result in having a better support system. Successful people know to accept the help and support of others!

4. PRACTICE. Whether learning to ride a bicycle, program a computer, play a musical instrument or use assertive behavior, intellectual comprehension of concepts is not all it takes! (Sorry, all you THINKERS). To become skillful with any behavior requires *practice*. A great deal of practice may be needed before a new behavior becomes natural and integrated.

- Decide what to practice and how it can best be accomplished.
- Develop a practice schedule. Be specific about how often, when and where. Record your efforts.
- Allow yourself to make mistakes. Remember, it is practice and you don't have to be perfect!

5. PROOF. When your practice goes well and you experience good feelings, you are receiving *proof* that you can change. This provides valuable *reinforcement* that encourages you to do it again. New behavior must be reinforced repeatedly with positive experiences (proof) to keep the process working and assure a permanent change.

- Ask others to give you positive feedback about your practice.
- Give yourself "pats on the back" with positive self-talk.
- Establish a practice schedule and reward yourself for keeping your commitment. Give yourself a reward just for practicing. You don't have to be completely changed to deserve some positive reinforcement.

ARE YOU USING THE RIGHT MAPS?

In the preface of this book you read that developing assertiveness requires THINKING assertively, FEELING confident and BEHAVING positively. In this section you will learn some ways to change your thinking—attitudes, expectations, beliefs and perceptions. As long as your thinking is non-assertive or aggressive, you will continue to choose those behaviors. Becoming assertive may require changing how you think about yourself, other people and life in general.

Practicing new behaviors is an important part of developing your assertiveness. Later you will receive specific suggestions that will help you practice. Before you begin to practice however, another important factor requires your attention. Your expectations about learning to be more assertive will have a strong influence on your success.

How Realistic Are Your Expectations?

Complete the following assessment to gain some insight about your expectations, then check your responses with those of the author.

AGREE or DISAGREE (A or D)

_____ 1. If people know too much about you they can use this information against you.

_____ 2. If everything is going smoothly, look out! Something is bound to go wrong soon.

_____ 3. There is a potential positive outcome to any problem or adverse situation.

_____ 4. If you want something done right you must do it yourself.

_____ 5. Bad luck comes in threes.

_____ 6. When you smile, the world smiles with you.

_____ 7. Everyone deserves recognition—not just those who excel.

_____ 8. The rich get richer and the poor get poorer.

_____ 9. It's okay to admit mistakes—people respect honesty.

_____ 10. New people, new situations and new experiences are fun and exciting.

If you agreed with #1, 2, 4 and 5 you are reflecting consistently negative expectations, particulary about people. If you agreed with #3, 6, 9 and 10 you have a positive outlook. If you agreed with #7 you appear to be generous and realistic. If you agreed with #2 and 8 you seem to feel you have little control over life.

SELF-FULFILLING PROPHECY

Have you ever heard of self-fulfilling prophecy? Whether you have or not, there is such a phenomenon. It often happens without our conscious awareness of its happening. Self-fulfilling prophecy is the phenomenon that results in our experiencing what we expect to experience. It is our getting from others just what we thought we would. We often succeed or fail because we subconsciously "knew" we would!

Our lives are full of examples of this phenomenon. Have you ever thought, "I'll never get this finished on time!" and then proved yourself right? Have you noticed that some people approach situations with an "I can't do this" attitude and experience problems and failures, while others approach the same situations with an "I can" attitude and succeed? Expectations and attitudes are powerful influences on actual outcomes.

A Case History

A brilliant young woman named Joyce was leaving home to attend college, but was concerned about her ailing mother. Her mother reassured Joyce and told her to go and be successful in her college studies. She said, "Don't worry dear. I'll live to see you graduate!"

Joyce went to college and performed at a superior level. During the first semester of her senior year she began to experience insomnia, loss of appetite and struggled with her studies. Her grades fell but she passed her courses. Her last semester was a disaster! Joyce's health continued to deteriorate and she dropped her two most difficult classes. This required attending another semester before she would graduate.

At the beginning of the next semester, Joyce's friends were concerned about her continued weight loss and general poor health. They encouraged her to seek help. Her doctor could find no explanation for her condition and arranged for her to meet with a psychologist. The psychologist uncovered Joyce's deep concern for her mother. The psychologist heard Joyce repeat her mother's pledge, "I'll live to see you graduate!" Her subconscious had interpreted that message as "I will die once you graduate." This simple phrase triggered an unconscious mechanism to delay graduation in order to keep her mother alive.

After counseling, Joyce was able to complete her courses and graduate with honors.

Do you believe in self-fulfilling prophecy? If not, you should, because it is a well-documented phenomenon. Controlled research has shown that teachers, trainers, managers, parents, etc., influence (often unintentionally) the behavior of their students, employees and/or children. Every day, subtle messages are delivered that communicate strong expectations.

Expectations, beliefs, attitudes and values are communicated constantly through our words, facial expressions, posture, eye contact, voice tones and behavior. Without intending to, we influence others and reinforce in them what we expect from them. Thus, we get just what we thought we would.

If you expect employees to complain, they will. If you expect them to be trustworthy and hard-working, they will be. It is what you *truly expect*, not what you say you want. It is not what you purport to believe in, but what you *really believe* that counts. Some managers say they have an "open door" but everyone knows their true message is "don't bother me." Parents may say, "We love you because you're you and a grade of B is fine." However, if mom and dad really want all As, their message will be communicated regardless of what they *say.*

How does this relate to being assertive? Assertive behavior comes more naturally when your core belief is that of an assertive philosophy. Whenever your expectations are nonassertive or aggressive, it is easy to send a double message when you wish to be assertive. Is there anything you can do? We think so. For openers you should read the following "Assertive Philosophy" often. Read it with conviction. Say the words aloud as though you sincerely believe them. If you genuinely wish to adopt a more assertive belief system, your perspective will begin to change and you will become more aware of the truth of the statements in your daily experience.

SELF-FULFILLING PROPHECY (continued)

An Assertive Philosophy

► I recognize that everyone has well-practiced communication habits and long-standing attitudes that support and defend these habits.

► I accept the communication habits of others as fact.

► I will offer assertive communication and a "win-win" attitude even when others are offering nonassertive or aggressive styles.

► I understand that people change only when they choose to change.

► I select my personal standard of communication rather than react to those of others.

► I know others are different from me and all kinds of people are OK.

► I accept responsibility for my feelings, thoughts, opinions and behavior. I realize I cannot be responsible for the feelings, thoughts, opinions and behaviors of others.

► I accept that every relationship involves each person having 50 percent of the responsibility for the success or failure of that relationship.

► I know that being nonassertive and aggressive is part of being human.

► I know that every assertive choice precludes a nonassertive or aggressive choice and improves the chances for success at work and at home.

Self-fulfilling prophecy has a flip side. When you deliver a speech knowing people will be interested and amused, sure enough, that's the way you experience it. But, if you are anxious about the crowd being bored and unresponsive, you very likely will have a miserable experience.

People who expect things to go wrong (i.e., who expect "foreigners" to be inhospitable, who expect to have no fun, who dread meeting strangers, etc.) invariably have such experiences again and again. To create positive outcomes you must start with positive expectations!

In the next section, you will learn about words and behaviors to practice to become more assertive. When you start practicing the new ways of expressing yourself and handling situations, it is a good idea to also practice the technique of "positive mental imagery."

Positive Mental Imagery is using your imagination to visualize yourself saying and doing things successfully and assertively. Envision situations where you *see* yourself *being* assertive. **Feel** confident, powerful and effective. **Hear** your voice sound strong and steady. **Experience** the satisfaction and pleasure of *being* assertive.

Do this repeatedly. Do it before you give a business presentation, before you ask an important question, before you introduce yourself to a stranger, etc. The more powerful your mental image and expectation, the greater the success you should experience.

Remember—only imagine positive outcomes. Don't think about the possibilities of things going badly, because your subconscious expectations are so powerful that envisioning failure could undermine your confidence and ultimate success. Recall the earlier situation of the student whose subconscious mind kept her from graduating because of a single powerful image planted years earlier.

Use the power of self-fulfilling prophecy to create positive experiences. When you are able to do this you have begun to develop an assertive philosophy. Think of positive mental imagery as programming a flight plan. Having the right expectations and perceptions before you start your journey is essential if you are going to reach your planned destination safely.

PROGRAMMING YOURSELF FOR SUCCESS

Positive Mental Imagery

Positive mental imagery is an exercise requiring conscious effort. It is a way to influence the subconscious mind. Subconscious expectations and internal dialogues are powerful influences on our perception of reality, our emotions and behaviors. Much of what exists in our subconscious was "recorded" in early life and can be thought of as a "psychological program."

Techniques to change both THINKING and FEELING patterns to help you become more assertive are explained in this section. You will learn to design a "psychological program" which will help support your conscious efforts.

Reprogramming Yourself

Much of our original "psychological programming" has been with us from childhood and prompts our nonassertive, assertive and/or aggressive behaviors. You cannot remove your original programming, but you can insert some new programming to counteract that which is problematic.

Unlike a computer, a person cannot be totally reprogrammed. With a computer, it is possible to create a new program and run it immediately. The computer does not have to "unlearn" old habits. With people, new programming must be done gradually and the new "program" must be "run" numerous times before things become automatic. But, it *can be done!*

How do you know what to put into your program? How do you enter the new programming? Review the quiz items on pages 3 and 15. These will help you recognize your beliefs, attitudes, perceptions or expectations that are not consistent with an assertive philosophy. Listening carefully to what you say and do can provide additional "shoulds" and "should nots" that are inconsistent with your being assertive. Keep a journal in which you record your thoughts and internal dialogue. Study it and it will reveal a number of old "programming messages" that you can change to improve your assertiveness.

To create a plan which will help you to reprogram yourself, write out new statements which will counteract old behaviors. This plan should include *Permissions* (It's OK to . . . , I can . . .), *Commitments* (I will . . .), and *Affirmations* (I am . . .). These statements must be written in **simple**, **active** and **positive** form. If they are complex, passive or negative, you will not get good results.

Start with only a few (4 or 5) reprogramming statements. Write each statement on a 3" × 5" index card. This size card is handy to carry with you in a pocket, purse or briefcase. To use the reprogramming cards most effectively, you should be relaxed. To achieve deep relaxation you can sit in a hot tub or take a bubble bath, listen to soothing music, rest after exercising vigorously or meditate. Once relaxed, read each card aloud several times—hear the words, believe then, let them sink into your relaxed mind.

Inserting ideas into your conscious, but highly relaxed mind will help you open your *subconscious* to receive the input. "Programs" are stored in our subconscious mind and you must "reprogram" your subconscious before it can support your new objectives. Read your cards regularly for several weeks to condition your mind. You can read your cards anytime for additional reinforcement, but using the "reprogramming" routine before sleep is particularly powerful because your subconscious is active periodically during sleep (that's why we dream). Your subconscious will absorb what your conscious mind heard before sleep if you use the routine regularly.

To review, the simple steps to reprogram yourself include:

- Write **simple, active, positive** statements that you want to record (one per card).

- Achieve a state of deep relaxation.

- Read each statement aloud several times.

- Sleep and let your subconscious absorb the ideas.

- Do this daily for 21 days.

PROGRAMMING YOURSELF FOR SUCCESS (continued)

Your statements should reflect your own objectives and needs. The most important statements are those that will help you change old patterns of thinking and behaving. You are the person who is best equipped to identify what you want and need to change, and to create a new program to support this change.

Sample Statements

Following are some sample statements. You may wish to use these (or others you create) for your initial "reprogramming."

It's OK for my wants and needs to be as important as those of others.
I can get my needs met.
I will ask for what I want.
I am someone who deserves having my needs met.

It's OK to have feelings and express them.
I can express my feelings openly and honestly.
I will tell others what I am feeling.
I am an emotionally honest person.

It's OK to make mistakes or not know something.
I can admit my mistakes or say "I don't know."
I will admit my mistakes and say "I don't know" when asked.
I am honest and will learn from my mistakes.
I can allow others to make mistakes.
I will have reasonable expectations of others.
I am realistic and understand that everyone makes mistakes.

It's OK to trust others.
I can share and trust.
I will trust and share.
I am a trusting and sharing person.

YOUR REPROGRAMMING STATEMENTS

Now that you have the idea, write some **simple**, **active**, **positive** statements for yourself. They can be any of the following forms. The Affirmations (I am . . .) probably are the most powerful, but your subconscious must believe these statements for them to work. Using permissions and commitments as a starting point may help.

Your Reprogramming Statements

Permissions:
It's OK to

It's OK to

It's OK to

Permissions:
I can

I can

I can

Commitments:
I will

I will

I will

Affirmations:
I am

I am

I am

Remember, don't use too many statements—only four or five initially. You have plenty of time to expand your behavior modification. Change is more effective one step at a time. This system *works* if you stick with it and give it an opportunity to work for you.

While reprogramming your subconscious each evening, you should also practice the new behaviors you desire on a daily basis. Part IV will help you learn how to do that.

III

Feelings: The Emotional Part of Assertiveness

THE EMOTIONS OF ASSERTIVENESS

Human beings are emotional creatures! All of us have feelings of some sort every waking moment. The emotional component of developing our assertiveness can be one of our most challenging undertakings. One reason for this is that most of us learn lessons about feelings that do not support assertiveness. A few of these lessons will be reviewed in this section and some new ideas will be put forth to help you learn to use your emotions as you develop your assertiveness.

One lesson transmitted in most cultures goes something like this: "Girls (women) are emotional; boys (men) are unemotional and rational." A true statement? Not really, everyone is emotional. Boys and men often don't learn about emotional honesty because they are taught early that they "aren't supposed to be emotional." Girls and women often learn exaggerated emotional responses to situations because they "are supposed to be emotional."

Another lesson is often labeled, "The Feeling Myth." Most of us grow up believing that people can make each other feel. For example, don't you believe that you can make someone angry? Do you worry about being assertive and "hurting someone's feelings"? This myth teaches us to believe that our words and actions literally cause other people to feel the emotions they feel. It teaches us to believe that we have no choice about our own feelings. It also teaches us to believe that we are responsible for one another's feelings.

Why is it called a myth? Because it is not true! Feelings are a choice. Most people don't believe that statement when they first hear it or read it. Further explanation may help you understand the truth of the statement.

ME? UPSET?

THE EMOTIONS OF ASSERTIVENESS (continued)

One way to understand that feelings are a choice is to think about cause and effect. If words, actions or events make someone angry, frightened or sad, the person has no choice. The person is made to feel that feeling. The word, action or event is the *cause* and the feeling is the *effect*. If the process truly were a cause-and-effect process, wouldn't it make sense that the same *cause* would then produce the same *effect* (feeling) in everyone? Simple observation proves that different people have different feelings about exactly the same event. Therefore it is the person receiving the words, actions or events who chooses an emotional response.

An Example: If someone decided to surprise you for a birthday by hiring someone in a clown suit to show up at your place of work and sing a song for you, how would you feel about the surprise? Whatever feeling you might have, you would probably agree that other people would respond differently to the same surprise. Some would be delighted and happy, others would feel embarrassed, others might get angry, and some might be disappointed. There is no sure way to predict anyone's emotional response in advance.

Granted, your emotional choice may be a strong habit. You might experience the same feeling in response to the same stimulus every time. This means you would perceive the process as being "made to feel." Realistically, you could choose a different emotional response even though it might feel unnatural at first.

Assertiveness demands emotional honesty. This is difficult to accomplish if you will not accept responsibility for your own feelings.

Another way to understand that we determine our feelings is to examine the process as an A B C system.

> A = Stimulus (word, behavior, event, etc.)
> B = Internal dialogue or self-talk
> C = Emotion

This whole process may happen in less than a second, but all three steps are always involved whenever we have an emotional response to something. Often it will seem that the feeling occurs simultaneously with the stimulus, but in a fraction of a second there was a sequence from A to C.

An Example: While working in his office a man was interrupted by the delivery of a telegram. He looked at the telegram and noticed that it was from the city where his ex-wife lived. Immediately he felt anger and threw it on his desk saying, "Why can't she just stay out of my life and let me live in peace!?"

Did the telegram make him angry? Many people would answer yes. Obviously he wasn't angry before he received the telegram and he got angry when he looked at it. Of course it made him angry.

What really happened was the A B C process. The man noticed the city of origin (A); assumed the telegram was from his ex-wife and that it contained some unwanted intrusion on his life (B); and then felt angry (C). His anger was in response to his thoughts. He could just as easily have felt guilty, sad, anxious or pleased.

To continue the story, the man opened the telegram. As soon as he read it, he whooped loudly, started laughing, jumped up from his desk and did an impromptu dance around his office. Why the sudden change in emotion?

The telegram was from a client. The message was: "Our board met today and considered your proposal. Thought you would like the news as soon as possible. We like your ideas and will double our business with you starting next month." Upon reading this message (A), the man was thinking about a trip to Hawaii and how much praise he would receive from his boss (B), and became very happy (C). It was the same telegram about which he first felt angry! The telegram did not make him mad or glad. His self-talk influenced his choice of feelings.

Another important reason for understanding the truth about feelings is to learn to use more of your power. By allowing others to "make you feel," you give the power to others. The old saying, "Sticks and stones may break my bones, but words can never hurt me," has an element of truth. Know that when you feel hurt, embarrassed, angry, sad or joyful, because of the words of others, you are *choosing* those feelings.

CHOICE AND WIN-WIN RELATIONSHIPS

Assertiveness is a win-win approach and philosophy. To build and maintain win-win relationships, each person must accept responsibility for his or her own feelings, thoughts and behaviors. You cannot be solely responsible for the feelings of others because you do not "make them feel." You are responsible for what you say and do because your words and actions *invite* others to feel certain emotions. Whether they do or not is up to them!

Assertiveness requires us to accept responsibility for our thoughts, feelings and behaviors and requires us to respect the thoughts, feelings and behaviors of others. When an individual accepts these responsibilities and stops blaming others for his or her feelings, a giant step has been taken toward a win-win philosophy.

What feeling would you choose? Why?

In the following exercise read the situation (A) and write your spontaneous emotion in the space under (C). Once you identify your feeling, write in what your self-talk was under (B).

Situation (A)	Self-talk (B)	Feeling (C)
A driver changes lanes without warning and almost hits your car.	_____ _____	_____
You are asked spontaneously by your boss to come forward at a company meeting and explain a project to 100 people.	_____ _____	_____
You finish an important presentation for your boss and important clients. When you return to your seat a colleague tells you that your shirt tail/blouse is sticking through an open zipper.	_____ _____	_____

Whatever feelings and self-talk you experienced for the situations on the preceding page are okay. There is nothing "bad" about feeling angry, embarrassed or elated. Your responses might not be the most productive or logical for the situation, but feelings are not logical. To change how you respond to certain situations, begin by changing your internal dialogue.

To practice this idea of learning new emotional responses by changing self-talk, use the same situations from the last exercise but create some different self-talk that will help you have a positive feeling.

Situation	Self-talk	Feeling
Near accident	_____	_____
	_____	
Speaking to 100 people	_____	_____
	_____	
Open zipper	_____	_____
	_____	

TALKING ABOUT FEELINGS

An important part of developing assertiveness is expressing your honest emotions. Many people don't do that. Even if you understand that being emotional is okay and part of being human, you may need practice to talk about your feelings. The assertive way to express feelings is to say "I feel . . . ," "I felt . . . ," "I'm feeling . . . ," "I am . . . ," "I was . . . ," "I get . . . ". What follows each phrase is a word describing a feeling.

First you must know what you are feeling. To figure out which emotion you are experiencing ask, "What am I feeling—**mad, sad, glad** or **scared**?" Those are the four basic human emotions and this question is a good one to help you get in touch with your feelings quickly and accurately. Some feelings are combinations of two or more of the four categories.

The following list may help you develop a vocabulary of emotions as you learn to express your feelings in a direct, open, honest manner.

mad	sad	glad	scared	combination
irritated	unhappy	pleased	anxious	guilty
annoyed	disappointed	happy	worried	jealous
angry	despondent	joyful	fearful	frustrated
ticked off	blue	delighted	concerned	embarrassed
furious	hurt	effervescent	afraid	uncomfortable
miffed	grief	comfortable	nervous	confused
upset	down	up	inhibited	perplexed
chapped	lonely	excited	uncertain	torn

You can add to the list. Because each person chooses and experiences feelings in a unique way, some feeling words will fit into different categories. Some people use "upset" to mean **mad** while others use it to mean **sad**. You decide the words that best reflect your feelings.

DEVELOPING EMOTIONAL AWARENESS

For the next week or two when you feel an emotion, stop and ask, "What am I feeling—mad, sad, glad, scared?" When you identify your feeling, make yourself aware of the underlying self-talk associated with it. Learn to recognize the physical symptoms related to that feeling. What signals accompany anger, fear, sadness and joy? Recognizing these physical clues will help you increase your emotional awareness. This is the first step toward expressing your feelings assertively.

In the next section on BEHAVIOR you will learn more about word choices to express not only your feelings, but also your opinions, thoughts, facts, etc. Other guidelines for assertive behavior will also be provided that will reinforce your assertive words.

P A R T

IV

Changing Your
Behaviors

CHOOSE ASSERTIVE WORDS CAREFULLY

Now that you have an understanding about how to change your THINKING and FEELING patterns, you need some information about changing BEHAVIOR.

To communicate thoughts, feelings and opinions assertively, you need to choose words that are direct, honest, appropriate and respectful. Some words simply do not fit these criteria and therefore cannot be delivered assertively. Words are only one aspect of being assertive, but you must have assertive words if you are to be assertive with others.

Guidelines for Assertive Word Choice

► **Use "I-statements" rather than "you-statements."**

Compare the following:

"You always interrupt my stories!" (Aggressive)
"I would like to tell my stories without interruption." (Assertive)

► **Use factual descriptions instead of judgments or exaggerations.**

Compare the following:

"If you don't change your attitude, you're going to be in real trouble." (Aggressive)
"If you continue to arrive after 8:00 a.m., I will be required to place you on 2 days' probation without pay." (Assertive)

► **Express thoughts, feelings and opinions reflecting ownership.**

Compare the following:

"He makes me angry!" (Denies ownership of feelings)
"I get angry when he breaks his promises!" (Assertive and owns feelings)

"The only sensible policy is to match the competition." (States *opinion* as fact; Aggressive, controlling)

"I believe matching the competition is the best policy." (Owns opinion; Assertive)

"Don't you think we should table this for now?" (Passive, indirect, denies ownership)

CHOOSE ASSERTIVE WORDS CAREFULLY (continued)

► **Use clear, direct requests or directives (commands) when you want others to do something rather than hinting, being indirect or presuming.**

Compare the following:

"Would you mind taking this to John?" (Indirect, only inquires about willingness)
"Will you please take this to John?" (Assertive request)
"Please take this to John." (Assertive directive)

"Why don't you stop on the way home and pick up milk?" (Indirect, asks the other to think about not doing it)
"Will you please pick up milk on your way home?" (Assertive request)
"Please pick up milk on your way home." (Assertive directive)

People avoid being direct and honest because they learned to think it was impolite or pushy. Unfortunately, while attempting to avoid being inappropriate we sometimes choose words that communicate a lack of respect. Sometimes we are so "careful" we don't communicate the real message.

When we say "don't you think" instead of "I think," we are communicating indirectly. If you really listen to the words, they sound condescending. When you ask "why don't you" instead of "will you," you are literally asking a person to find reasons not to. When you say "I need," and presume someone will take care of your needs, you communicate a lack of respect or an air of superiority. If you say "I need" or "I want," learn to add a request or directive in order to be assertive.

These may seem like "picky" details. You might say, "Most people know what is meant when I use those words, so what's the difference?" The difference is that you may be getting expected results only because people are able to figure out your unexpressed intentions. You may not be getting their respect. Continuing to use improper words will reinforce old habits and interfere with your being truly assertive. You can increase your success rate and improve relationships by using the direct, honest, assertive words.

SOME DOs AND DON'Ts

Following are some DO's and DON'Ts for Assertive word selection.

DO	**DON'T**
Say "no" politely and firmly	Say "I can't" or "I won't be able to."
Express feelings honestly: "I'm angry" "I'm disappointed" "I'm delighted" "I enjoy being with you"	Depersonalize feelings or deny ownership: "You make me mad" "That's disappointing" "That's delightful" "You make me feel so good"
Be realistic, respectful and honest:	Exaggerate, minimize or use sarcasm:
SAY "This is the third straight month your report has been late."	SAY "You are never on time with your reports."
SAY "Thank you for asking. I prefer no smoking in my car."	SAY Uh, okay. We wouldn't want to strain your will power!"
Express preferences and priorities:	Don't defer to be sociable or agree unwillingly:
SAY "I don't have a particular movie to suggest. I do want to avoid ones with violence."	SAY "I don't care–whatever everyone else wants is okay with me."

Time To Practice

With the above guidelines fresh in mind, write some assertive words on a sheet of paper that are appropriate for the following situations:

1. You did not understand what someone just told you and want her to restate her message.

2. You believe you deserve a raise and decide to ask your boss directly.

3. You have been invited to a social event that does not interest you. Decline the invitation.

4. You are pleased about what someone has done. Tell him your feelings.

A quick self-check question is: "What do these words invite from the other?" This will help you determine if they are assertive, aggressive or nonassertive.

BODY-LANGUAGE SIGNALS

We have now seen that your word choice is critically important. Perhaps even more essential is how you say them. Your delivery of the message makes all the difference. Most people use the phrase "body language" to refer to all aspects of interpersonal communication beyond the choice of words. Everything becomes important when a message is being delivered: voice tone, volume, inflection, pace, eye contact or lack of it, facial expression, gestures, movements or lack thereof, posture, muscle tension, changes in skin coloring, clothing, hair style, eyeglasses, etc. Whew!

Staying aware of all aspects of body language continuously is not possible. Having some awareness is very important in your assertiveness training. Even though other people might not be able to list all of your body-language signals during an interaction, they respond and interpret them unconsciously as part of receiving your message. This process is automatic, constant and complex.

Don't be discouraged. You don't have to constantly monitor all aspects of body language to be assertive. You do, however, need to learn some body-language signals to accompany your words that will help you be perceived as an assertive person. Perfection is not required for success.

On the next page are some basic body-language signals that have been categorized according to how most people perceive them. As you read the list, you may want to act out each one to get a better sense of what the signal communicates.

NONASSERTIVE	ASSERTIVE	AGGRESSIVE

Posture

slumped	erect but relaxed	erect, tense, rigid
shoulders forward	shoulders straight	shoulders back
shifting often	few shifts, comfortable	jerky shifts or planted in place
chin down	head straight or slight tilt	chin up or thrust forward
sitting: legs entwined	sitting: legs together or crossed	sitting: heels on desk, hands behind head or tensely leaning forward

Gestures

fluttering hands	casual hand movements	chopping or jabbing with hands
twisting motions	relaxed hands	clenched hands or pointing
shoulder shrugs	hands open, palms out	sweeping arms
frequent head nodding	occasional head nodding	sharp, quick nods

Facial Expression

lifted eyebrows, pleading look, wide-eyed, rapid blinking	relaxed, thoughtful, caring or concerned look, few blinks	furrowed brow, tight jaw tense look, unblinking glare patronizing or sarcastic smile
nervous or guilty smile	genuine smile	tight lips
chewing lower lip	relaxed mouth	shows anger with disapproving scowl, very firm mouth or bared teeth, extreme flush
shows anger with averted eyes, blushing, guilty look	shows anger with flashing eyes, serious look, slight flush of color	

Voice

quiet, soft, higher pitch	resonant, firm, pleasant	steely quiet or loud, harsh
uhs, ahs, hesitations	smooth, even-flowing	"biting off" words, precise measured delivery
stopping in "midstream"	comfortable delivery	sarcastic laughter
nervous laughter	laughter only with humor	statements sound like orders or pronouncements
statements sound like questions with voice tone rising at the end	voice tones stay even when making statement	

BODY-LANGUAGE SIGNALS (continued)

Nonassertive, Assertive or Aggressive?

Given the list of Body-Language Signals on the previous page, how would you classify the following?

NAS = Nonassertive   AS = Assertive   AG = Aggressive

_____ **1.** Elbows out, fists on hips

_____ **2.** Touching someone's forearm as you speak with them

_____ **3.** While walking, putting an arm around someone's shoulders and firmly grasping their shoulder on side opposite you

_____ **4.** Shifting repeatedly from one foot to the other while standing

_____ **5.** Constantly nodding head up and down

_____ **6.** Leaning back, propping feet on desk, grasping hands behind head

_____ **7.** Looking at toes while speaking

_____ **8.** Leaning forward with hands grasped, elbows on knees while seated facing someone

_____ **9.** Rapidly tapping pencil (like a drumstick) while listening

_____ **10.** Sitting with elbows on table, hands together, chin on hands while listening

_____ **11.** Standing with arms folded while listening

_____ **12.** Standing with arms folded, head tilted and legs crossed

_____ **13.** Looking over the tops of eyeglasses

_____ **14.** Twirling a pencil with fingers at each end while talking

_____ **15.** Elbows on table, hands together at fingertips forming a "steeple"

Author's Answers

1. Aggressive. This posture makes a person look larger, much like birds fluff feathers, mammals raise neck hairs and some fish and reptiles inflate themselves.

2. Assertive. This may be a comforting gesture or a way to communicate emphasis.

3. Aggressive. This entraps the other person and is a controlling maneuver rather than an affectionate or comforting one.

4. Nonassertive. The shifting movement communicates anxiety.

5. Nonassertive. Head bobbing usually signals, "I want to please you." Occasional nods may communicate attentiveness.

6. Aggressive. Most people perceive this as a power display.

7. Nonassertive. Looking down frequently or steadily communicates anxiety.

8. Assertive. This probably will signal interest and attentiveness.

9. Aggressive. When the tapping communicates impatience or boredom—it might come across as nervousness (accompanying signals make the difference).

10. Assertive. This looks relaxed and attentive.

11. Aggressive. This is the most frequent interpretation. Others include "closed mind," impatient, bored, uncaring and defensive.

12. Nonassertive. This posture usually signals deference and it is almost impossible to stay still. It could appear relaxed with a peer.

13. Aggressive. This signal usually looks disapproving or threatening.

14. Nonassertive. Twirling the pencil probably communicates anxiety. Doing it while listening to someone could signal impatience.

15. Aggressive. This is another subtle power display.

The above answers represent the most common interpretation of the signals.

BODY-LANGUAGE SIGNALS (continued)

It is important to understand that body-language signals have many possible interpretations. A single body-language cue is often not enough for an accurate "reading" of the communication. Body language signals must be interpreted in total. Much like a detective, it is necessary to discover and interpret a number of clues to solve the "body-language mystery."

One way to become more sensitive to body language is to become a "people watcher with a purpose." This can help you develop a better awareness of how body language communicates nonassertive, assertive and aggressive behaviors. You will notice that people not only use different words with each style, but also communicate these styles with their body-language signals. Recognizing nonassertive and aggressive signals can help you learn to avoid using them when your goal is to be perceived as assertive.

One way to develop your assertiveness is to find an assertive person and observe this person's behavior. Take note of the words and body language the person uses. Most of what we learned as children was through observation. The system still works. Following a good role model is an easy and fun way to learn how to become more assertive.

A Case History

Body language makes a difference! Jurors are often influenced by the body language of the opposing attorneys and witnesses. In a recent personal injury case, the attorney representing the plaintiff strutted, smirked and used a loud, nasal voice while questioning witnesses. When the defense attorney would comment or ask questions, the plaintiff's attorney would make disbelieving or disapproving facial expressions.

The defense attorney was not a strong personality. He spoke in a quiet voice. He slumped when he sat and walked with poor postures. His movements were jerky and uncertain.

The jury seemed offended by the behavior of the plaintiff's attorney. On the other hand, they were not impressed with the defendant's attorney. Without knowing any of the evidence in the case, can you predict which attorney won?

Obviously, the evidence and testimony were factors; however the consistently obnoxious behavior of the plaintiff's attorney was the key factor. The jurors were so annoyed by his aggressiveness toward the witnesses that they decided for the defense. A respectful, assertive attorney could have won for the plaintiff.

STOP SIGNS AND GREEN LIGHTS

Stop Signs

There are several signals that will indicate when you are headed down the wrong road. These signals can be either nonassertive or aggressive. Read and learn the signals. Practice using what you learn. It's okay to stop and say something like "Excuse me. Let me start over." Others will respect your efforts to be assertive.

 Saying "you should," "you must," "you have to." Restate as either a request or directive.

 Using exaggerated words—"obviously," "absolutely," "always," "never," "impossible." Restate with more realistic and factual words.

 Saying "ya' know," "maybe," "kinda," "sorta," "only," "just," "I guess." Restate in a more direct, confident manner without the wishy-washy qualifiers.

 Asking "can you," "could you," "would you," "why don't you," "would you mind," "do you think you might." Request by asking "will you please"—it is the only question that truly asks for action and a commitment!

 Using "it," "that," "one," "you," "we" instead of "I." State your thoughts with "I think," your opinions with "I believe," and your feelings with "I feel (mad, sad, glad, scared)" or "I am (mad, sad, glad, scared)."

STOP SIGNS AND GREEN LIGHTS
(continued)

Green Lights

The following signals indicate you are on the right road and communicating assertively. Keep going when you have green lights!

 When you feel relaxed, comfortable and stress free. These are positive signs that you are being assertive.

 When the person with whom you are interacting displays attentiveness, comfort, cooperation and respect. When you see no signals of bad feelings, rebellion, disregard or defensiveness, you are being assertive.

 When another says "okay," "sure" or "I'll be glad to" in response to your request or directive. When others do what you wanted with no indication of resentment or discomfort, you have good evidence you were assertive.

 When others are assertive with you. When they communicate their honest thoughts, feelings, opinions, wants and needs in a direct and respectful manner, they are affirming your assertive behavior with them.

P A R T

V

Expanding Your Assertiveness

FOUR ASSERTIVE STYLES

Everyone has a natural assertive style which comes from his or her basic personality. You probably will recognize yours as you read the following four descriptions.

► **SUPPORTING/CARING**

This style communicates warmth, nurturing and concern for others. Content is presented in a direct, honest and respectful manner. It maintains an awareness for the feelings of others. Those who naturally use this assertive style are often FEELERS.

► **DIRECTING/GUIDING**

This is an impersonal style that communicates a no-nonsense, authoritative approach and a concern for results. It is a firm but respectful style using directives rather than requests. It does not come across as being "bossy" or "dictatorial." The Directing/Guiding style communicates beliefs and opinions appropriately as well as commands. Those who use this style most frequently are DOERS and/or THINKERS.

► **ANALYTICAL**

This style also is impersonal and matter-of-fact. It communicates facts, information, thoughts and probabilities. This style uses requests to obtain results rather than directives. Directing/Guiding is a "tell 'em" style while Analytical is an "ask 'em" style. Analytical is calm and emotionless. It is used most naturally by those in the THINKER group.

► **EXPRESSIVE**

This style is animated, energetic, spontaneous and emotional. Feelings, likes and dislikes, wants and needs are communicated in this style in an open and expressive manner. Those using this style are usually intuitive, creative, spontaneous and lively. They are normally DOERS or FEELERS.

Did you recognize your natural assertive style? Did you recognize others you know as you read each description? All four styles are assertive because each communicates in an appropriate, direct and honest manner.

WHICH STYLE IS WHICH?—A QUIZ

Using the abbreviations listed below, identify which assertive style is used in the following examples. You can check your answers below. Reading them aloud may help you recognize the differences.

S/C = Supporting/Caring   D/G = Directing/Guiding   A = Analytical   E=Expressive

_____ 1. "The quarterly report indicates a 7 percent increase in productivity."

_____ 2. "Hey! That's terrific!"

_____ 3. "I really appreciate your summarizing all that data for us."

_____ 4. "It's important to nail down just how that was accomplished."

_____ 5. "Give me some more details on that new product line."

_____ 6. "I know you're excited about our new products, Pat, and I would like to hear more about them after we finish the productivity discussion."

_____ 7. "Thank you Terry. I estimate about 20 minutes will be required to complete the productivity analysis. The next item on the agenda will be new products."

_____ 8. "Okay, let's do it. This productivity stuff is boring and I'd like to get on to a new topic!"

_____ 9. "Chris, you sure like the new ideas, don't you? Thank you for being patient and keeping a lid on long enough for us to finish."

_____ 10. "My analysis revealed three factors that contributed to the productivity improvement. The first was . . ."

ANSWERS

1. **A**—A straightforward statement of facts.
2. **E**—Spontaneous enthusiasm.
3. **S/C**—A personal acknowledgment with gratitude.
4. **D/G**—A statement of opinion and a concern for results.
5. **D/G**—Commanding someone to provide information.
6. **S/C**—Recognizing another's interest and indicating support while preventing a diversion.
7. **A**—Providing information about timing and upcoming agenda item.
8. **E**—Action words, stating a dislike and enthusiasm for the suggested new topic.
9. **S/C**—Acknowledging Chris's enthusiasm and expressing appreciation for cooperation.
10. **A**—Informative, factual, unemotional.

A Case History

A Directing/Guiding manager, Joyce had an administrative assistant, Sue, who was a Supporting/Caring person. Sue wanted to help Joyce and was dedicated to doing everything possible to maintain a satisfying relationship. Joyce was unconcerned about the quality of the relationship and concentrated more on getting things done.

Over time, Joyce's continued use of directives began to create stress for Sue. Like most Supporting/Caring people, Sue interpreted commands as uncaring and occasionally heard them as reprimands. Sue's interest in Joyce's family and home life seemed unprofessional to Joyce and was a source of discomfort.

After months of working together, Sue resigned. In the exit interview conducted by the Director of Personnel, Sue explained that her manager seemed to disapprove of her many efforts to help. Sue said she was leaving to find a job with a boss who would appreciate qualities such as loyalty, devotion and anticipation of needs.

When the Director of Personnel reviewed the interview with Joyce, the result was amazed perplexity. Joyce explained how her assistant always wanted to talk about families and seemed to hover about, expressing concern about not being able to help more. "I don't like someone fussing over me all the time. I want my employees to do what I tell them and concentrate on doing their work."

It is obvious to an informed observer how the manager and assistant failed to understand each other's priorities and style. When those involved don't know about differences in personality styles, they often fail to communicate and will experience stressful relationships.

By learning to recognize and use the four assertive styles, you will be able to communicate more effectively with almost everyone. Once you recognize a style and sensitively match it (at least part of the time) you will improve your communication with that person—even if it was previously difficult to make a connection. An easy way to remember the importance of matching styles is to think of speaking with someone by short-wave radio. If you send your message on one channel and she receives on another channel, you will not be able to communicate. When you are both on the same channel, then you can communicate.

SENDING ASSERTIVE MESSAGES

Following is an exercise that will allow you to practice sending messages in different styles. Write your responses and then compare your basic usage with the sample provided. **Important**—Do not look at the samples before writing your message. The purpose of this exercise is to practice using what you have learned. If you need help, look at the examples at the beginning of the chapter. Your words do not have to be the same—but the meaning should be similar.

MESSAGE: Tell or ask Pat to assist you with a project.

Supporting/Caring Style:

Directing/Guiding Style:

Analytical Style:

Expressive Style:

MESSAGE: Give Chris feedback about how well she has organized a meeting.

Supporting/Caring Style:

Directing/Guiding Style:

Analytical Style:

Expressive Style:

(See sample responses on the facing page)

COMPARE YOUR RESPONSES

Sample Responses: Compare your messages with the following examples. Yours may not be exactly like the samples but they should help you judge how successfully you were able to "switch channels." Remember, it is not simply the choice of words that create a style. Read your messages aloud with appropriate delivery to help you communicate in the different styles.

SUPPORTING/CARING: "Pat, if you can spare the time, will you please give me some help on this project? Thank you so much."

DIRECTING/GUIDING: "Pat, please complete this part for me so I can wrap up this project."

ANALYTICAL: "Pat, if you assist me, I can complete this project this week. Will you organize this section?"

EXPRESSIVE: "Pat! Help! I'm swamped—how about running some figures for me?"

SUPPORTING/CARING: "Chris, I really appreciate how well you organized the conference. Everyone seemed comfortable with the arrangements."

DIRECTING/GUIDING: "Chris, that was a fine job on the meeting arrangements."

ANALYTICAL: "Chris, your arrangements for the conference were very complete. The sessions were on time, everyone had all the necessary information and the meeting ran efficiently."

EXPRESSIVE: "Super job, Chris! Great meeting!"

CAN YOU IDENTIFY THESE PEOPLE?

Two business people were seated in the same row in an airplane. The middle seat was initially empty. It was a full flight and a third person finally occupied the seat between the two travelers. The person in the middle was a man who also appeared to be traveling for business.

The person by the window asked the man in the middle, "What is your destination?" The man answered, "Chicago." After a short while the passenger by the window asked, "What business are you in?" The reply, "Electronics." The person by the window made no further attempts to communicate.

The person sitting in the aisle seat had heard the above interaction. This passenger also noticed the middle passenger's expensive suit, costly wristwatch and eelskin briefcase. Assessing the visual clues and lack of responsiveness to the other person's questions, the aisle passenger said to the man in the middle seat, "Tell me about what you do." The man launched into a lengthy explanation of his business, the purpose of the trip and his past successes!

1. Which communication style was used by the window seat passenger?

2. Which style was used by the aisle seat passenger?

3. What was the middle passenger's personality type? (THINKER, FEELER or DOER)

When the aisle passenger correctly assessed the middle seat passenger as a DOER who did not respond to the Analytical style, this provided information about which style would be successful. Many DOERS use a Directing/Guiding style and exhibit pride in what they have achieved with visible signs of success. Using a directive aimed at "doing" established rapport instantly. The Analytical communicator had no success involving the middle seat passenger in conversation because an inaccurate choice of words was used.

ANSWERS:

1. Analytical   2. Directing/Guiding   3. Doer

HOW DELIVERY AFFECTS DIFFERENT STYLES

How you say words is important when using each style. Following are some suggestions for successful delivery:

SUPPORTING/CARING: Use a warm, nurturing, mellow tone of voice. Communicate personal interest, appreciation, concern, gratitude or empathy by making good eye contact and using comforting facial expressions (think of a loving grandparent).

DIRECTING/GUIDING: Be firm and authoritative, but not harsh or dictatorial. Your delivery should be matter of fact, direct and serious. Facial involvement is an expression of concentration or purpose.

ANALYTICAL: Use an even, no-nonsense, pragmatic delivery. Your facial expression looks alert and thoughtful. You can be polite, but don't show emotion.

EXPRESSIVE: Everything is expressive! Your voice range and facial expressions are almost limitless. Be animated with your face, hands and body movements. Show emotion.

ROLE MODELS can help you learn to use all four assertive styles. As mentioned earlier, it is fun to follow the example of someone whose natural style is one of the four assertive styles. Very likely you have mentally identified someone with a similar style to each of the types described. If not, you should be able to find one of each by listening and observing. It is also possible to find examples of the four assertive styles in television programs or movies. Once you find a role model of the style you want to practice, study that person and adopt those characteristics that seem most effective.

IDENTIFY STYLES TO ENHANCE COMMUNICATION

To identify people who fit into one personality group or the other, look for the characteristics described below. Once you have figured out what someone's dominant personality type is, you can communicate more effectively with that person by using the matching assertive style.

▶ **SUPPORTING/CARING:** These people value relationships and work hard at maintaining them. They often do thoughtful things, show awareness of and concern for others. They are comfortable with self-disclosure and will talk about personal issues. Supporting/Caring people will ask about you and your family. They have a comfortable look about them with comfortable clothes, an open posture and a kind, gentle facial expression. Their offices will have touches of home with family photographs, plants and a comfortable seating arrangement. Supporting/Caring people need personal recognition and evidence that you care about them (not just their work).

▶ **DIRECTING/GUIDING:** These people value results, accomplishments, action, loyalty and other important things (according to what they define as important). They are not comfortable with self-disclosure and will usually talk about work, projects and things, while rarely revealing anything about themselves other than their achievements and activities. They are not particularly interested in hearing about you, your family or your problems. They prefer to keep things impersonal. Directing/Guiding people have a serious, almost stern, look about them with closed postures and a military bearing. Their offices are a serious, organized places where things get done, and there are few personal touches other than symbols of their accomplishments or their beliefs and values. The seating arrangement is formal and distancing.

▶ **ANALYTICAL:** These people value information, accuracy, logical thinking and organization. They have a great need for structure and schedules and tend to be perfectionists. Like Directing/Guiding people, they prefer to keep things impersonal and will not reveal much about themselves except to share ideas. They reveal the least amount of emotion of any of the personality types and have an almost expressionless look about them most of the time. Analytical people may be obsessively neat and organize, or they may have so much information, data, manuals, reports, etc., in their offices that there will be stacks everywhere. They do have systems for what appears to be clutter, and they can find what they need. If there is seating for guests in their offices, it may be covered with piles of information.

► **EXPRESSIVE:** These people value excitement, stimulation, fun, spontaneity and attention. They are the most animated and openly emotional of the four types of people. They are self-disclosing and talk about themselves a lot. They draw attention to themselves with bright colors, flamboyant dress or behavior, or with their creativity and humor. Expressive people have toys in their offices, color, art, music and (if they can get away with it) unusual seating arrangements and personal touches. They display a wide range of facial expressions and react quickly and often dramatically to what others say and do.

Remember—all four types of people are okay! They each have their own communication style, values, strengths and weaknesses, and they each have the potential to be consistently assertive in their own way. People tend to think of their own type as the best and view the others as inferior, but that kind of thinking is not consistent with the assertive philosophy you are learning to follow. Learn to recognize each type so you can effectively communicate with them and put self-fulfilling prophecy to work by concentrating on their positive characteristics.

As you practice matching the style of each type of person, you will be developing your own underlying strengths. You will find that matching styles becomes easier, and you will become aware of new abilities, perceptions and characteristics emerging in yourself. What a nice bonus from learning to communicate more effectively with others!

P   A   R   T

VI

Assertive Power Steps

FOUR STEPS TO ASSERTIVE COMMUNICATION

Even if you successfully choose assertive words, correctly assess the other person's personality type and the style of assertiveness to which they might best respond, and deliver your words with the appropriate body language, there is no guarantee that the other person will respond with the desired cooperative response! You never have more than 50 percent of the control in any human interaction, and the other person may ignore your skillful assertiveness.

This is when you need to be prepared to increase the power of your assertiveness. You continue to be assertive, but you become a little more insistent, a little more emotional or a little more commanding to be sure that you get what you want in the situation. Think of it as "power steps"—you start at the bottom step, which is basic assertive behavior, and if that does not work, you take one step up in power. If that does not work, you take another step and another, if needed. At no point do you have to resort to aggressive behavior.

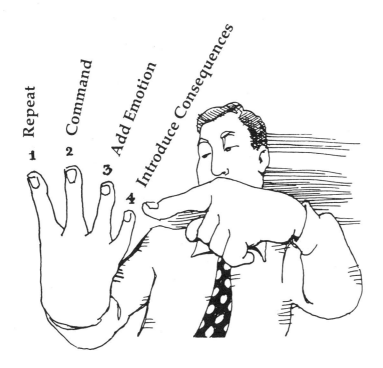

FOUR STEPS TO ASSERTIVE COMMUNICATION (continued)

STEP 1: Repeat the Question or Statement

One way to add power to your assertiveness is to repeat your first communication. Some have referred to this tactic as the "broken record." You ask the same question or make the same statement. Make sure that you have good eye contact and that you speak with confident, assertive voice tones. You may want to emphasize certain words the second time to increase the chances of getting your point across.

Assertive statement: "Will you please tell me how to find Mr. Green's office?" (No response from the other person)

Assertive statement: "Will you **please** tell me how to find Mr. Green's office?"

STEP 2: Command, Don't Ask

If the other person continues to ignore you or refuses to cooperate, switch from asking to commanding. To most people a directive sounds more powerful than a request. Because this is true, we recommend in our training programs that you learn to use the request for the majority of people (the most notable exception being the Directing/Guiding type of person). The average person will hear your request as polite and appropriate, there is less risk of sounding pushy and you can change to a command if the request does not produce results.

Assertive statement: "Please give me directions to Mr. Green's office."

Before we consider other ways to increase the power of your assertiveness, it is time for you to practice escalating your assertiveness just a little when your first effort is not successful.

> ## *Situation #1*
>
> *You are participating in a staff meeting and want to make a point about the topic being discussed. Assume a topic and write your assertive statement below:*
>
> _____
>
> *Alas, no one responds. Perhaps they have not heard you, or they may be choosing to ignore you. If you are going to repeat the original statement, write below which words you would emphasize to add a small amount of power.*
>
> _____
>
> *Still no one responds! Write below what you would say to be even more emphatic about your point without becoming aggressive.*
>
> _____
>
> _____
>
> *Now ask someone to evaluate your practice efforts to verify that you have been assertive each time.*

STEP 3: Add Emotion

If your efforts are still unsuccessful, you can express your emotions as another way to add power to your assertiveness. People are unaccustomed to others expressing emotion openly and honestly, and by doing so you add considerable power to your communication.

Assertive statement: "I suggest that we bring in a consultant to help us with this." (No response from the others)

Assertive statement: "**I suggest** that we bring in a consultant **to help us** with this." (Still no response)

Assertive statement: "Please tell me what you think of my suggestion to bring in a consultant to help us." (No response or a dismissive response)

Assertive statement: "**Now I'm getting angry! Please give me a serious response to my suggestion.**"

FOUR STEPS TO ASSERTIVE COMMUNICATION (continued)

You will probably get some attention with the last one! This level of assertiveness would be inappropriate earlier in the process, but after three attempts to be heard it is quite appropriate. It not only will result in respectful attention but will likely produce apologies from the others. You do not have to apologize for expressing your emotions, and it is recommended that you do not. You are completely within your rights to respond emotionally if you do not receive respectful responses from others when you are making a serious effort to communicate assertively. Apologies will only diminish your power. If you do receive the response you desired, it would be a good idea to express appreciation.

Situation #2

Assume that you are asking someone to assist you with a task or project or that you are asking for another person's ideas or preferences. Write your request below.

_____

_____

Assume that you get no response or an insincere one. Write a command version below.

_____

_____

Assume that this second effort receives no better response. Write an assertive communication in which you express your feelings about the situation.

_____

_____

Now ask someone to evaluate your practice efforts to be sure that you have been assertive each time.

You may be tempted by now to become aggressive in order to get your needs met, but please do not yield to this temptation. By remaining assertive you have a better chance of getting cooperation without the risk of retaliation. When you do use aggression to get your way, you must be prepared to receive aggression in return from the person whose rights you violated!

STEP 4: Introduce Consequences

A final way to add power to your assertiveness is to introduce consequences. Consequences are not threats, because they are not harmful or inappropriate. They are simply statements of what you intend to do if you do not get the cooperation or results you desire. Listed below are some criteria for successful consequences.

- Consequences need to be stated in advance. The other person deserves an opportunity to change his or her behavior to prevent the consequence. Taking the action without prior notice could be interpreted as inappropriate and aggressive.

- Consequences need to be strong but believable. The action needs to be something that the other person does not want to experience, but if it is too extreme the other person will not believe that you will actually do it. Empty threats are ignored.

- You must be prepared to follow through and implement the consequence if necessary. If the other person decides to test you and you do not take the action you said you would, you will lose credibility and power for dealing with this person in the future. He or she may also tell others, and you will lose credibility with them, too.

Some Examples

After several attempts to get someone to stop taking things from your desk without permission:

"If you take anything else from my desk without asking first, I will inform the department manager and the security office about this repeated pattern."

After you have asked one of your car pool drivers to stay within the speed limit and to stop following cars too closely:

"Pat, I really am uncomfortable with your driving so fast and following other cars so closely. If you continue to do this I will drop out of the car pool."

FOUR STEPS TO ASSERTIVE
COMMUNICATION (continued)

Situation #3

Assume that you have purchased an expensive new suit. The purchase price included alterations. You were in a hurry and did not try on the suit. When you put it on the next day, you discovered that the sleeves were still a little too long, there were a couple of wrinkles across the shoulders and the waist was a little loose. You have decided to return the suit for additional alteration and expect this additional tailoring to be free. How will you word your original request?

_____

_____

Assume that you are told that additional alterations will cost another $35.00. What will you say to get the store representative to provide the alterations at no charge?

_____

_____

_____

Assume that this effort falls on deaf ears. The sales person informs you that the store's policy requires that additional alterations after the customer has accepted the clothing be paid for, and he (or she) does not have the authority to break this rule. What will you say?

_____

_____

_____

Assume that this third attempt is not successful. Write a statement of consequences in the space below.

_____

_____

_____

Author's Statements

> *"When I put on my new suit I discovered several things about the fit that are not quite satisfactory, and I have brought it back so you can fix them. Will you please take care of it for me?"*
>
> *"My understanding was that alterations were included in the price and that a good fit was guaranteed, so I will appreciate your making these few small adjustments without charge."*
>
> *"When I picked up the suit I explained that I did not have time to try it on, and I was informed that would be no problem. If I had tried it on then I would not have accepted the suit as it is. If you cannot authorize additional alterations without charge, please get someone who can."*
>
> *"If you will not get your supervisor to authorize this and if you insist on charging me for additional alteration, I will not shop here in the future. I will inform the Better Business Bureau about the incident, and I will also inform the Consumer Hotline program of Channel 8 television."*

Remember that the whole idea of being assertive is to create win-win outcomes. By being patient and persistent with people while adding small increments of power to your communication efforts, you have a better chance of getting what you want while allowing the other person to feel respected. Their respect for you will grow as well, which will make future negotiations with this person even easier. Most people prefer dealing with others who know how to be powerful without being intimidating, rude or manipulative.

With practice, your skills for adding power will improve and your confidence and self-esteem* will grow. As your confidence and self-esteem develop, you will find that being assertive becomes even easier.

---

* To help you develop self-esteem, read *Developing Self-Esteem* by Connie Palladino and *Self-Empowerment* by Sam Lloyd and Tina Berthelot, also published by Crisp Publications, Inc.

P A R T

VII

Assertive Confrontation

DEFINING THE PROBLEM

Possibly the most challenging time to be assertive is when another person's behavior is unacceptable to you and you need to talk with this person about changing the behavior. What do you think of when you hear the word "confrontation"? Do you envision yelling and screaming? Do you imagine anger, tears, blame and accusation, denials and hurt feelings? Most people have only unpleasant experiences involving confrontation and have no idea how confrontation can be handled assertively, even caringly.

One important aspect of handling confrontation assertively is to define the problem in such a way that you can talk with the other person about the problem without communicating disapproval or disrespect. This requires that you learn to define the specific behavior that you find unacceptable rather than seeing the other person as unacceptable. This may take some practice!

With each example below, write in the "label" that someone might use to describe the person or the person's attitude or motivation. This is what most people do—label the other person—and this labeling is one of the reasons why a confrontation attempt may fail. After identifying the label that seems to fit the person, write a description of the specific behavior without using any judgmental words or personal adjectives.

Terry, a teenager, comes to the dinner table, takes a seat, looks at the meal that is on the table, rolls his eyes toward the ceiling and says,"I can't believe we're having this again! Don't you have any imagination? This is the most boring food in town!"

What label describes Terry? _____

What is the specific behavior? _____

_____

DEFINING THE PROBLEM (continued)

Rosa arrives for the 8:00 a.m. staff meeting at about 8:15 and, while avoiding eye contact with the others, finds an empty chair. While she is arranging several folders of materials and searching through her purse for something else, she knocks over her coffee cup. She grabs for the folders to save them from the coffee, and the contents of the folders fly everywhere. Rosa utters an expletive, collapses into her chair and buries her face in her hands.

What label describes Rosa? _____

What is the specific behavior?_____

_____

The labels are easier than the behavior descriptions, aren't they? Most of us have been judging and labeling others since we were children, so learning to factually describe specific behavior does take practice.

Author's Answers

Terry could be described as insolent, sullen, disrespectful or insubordinate, among other things. The specific behavior is making disparaging remarks about the meal.

Rosa could be described as tardy, disorganized, clumsy or uncommunicative. The specific behavior is arriving at 8:15 for an 8:00 meeting, spilling coffee and dropping papers while attempting to save them from the coffee.

In each of these cases it would be appropriate for the others involved to confront the behavior. The challenge is to confront the specific behavior rather than the person. If people feel they are being attacked, they will respond defensively and refuse to cooperate. If they hear that they are being judged, they will respond defensively and probably judge in return.

FIVE TOOLS FOR SUCCESSFUL CONFRONTATION

To resolve situations such as these, the confronter needs to approach the problem with the objective of informing the other person about the behavior, and the results of that behavior, in such a way that the person will feel respected and will be more likely to respond cooperatively. The following tools will help you learn to confront in just this manner.

1. **Identify which assertive style will work best.** Which type of personality will you be addressing? The confrontation will be more successful if you use the other person's natural style. The Analytical style is recommended for both the Analytical and the Directing/Guiding types of people. A directive approach is a little strong for confrontational situations.

2. **Define the specific behavior to be confronted.** Identify what the other does that you wish they did not do, or what they do not do that you wish they did. Define what they do differently from the way you would prefer. Avoid using judgmental or accusatory words. Be factual.

   Example: Factual descriptions of the behaviors from the two examples above—arriving after the starting time, making disparaging remarks.

   Practice: Use a current or recent problem situation in your own life that involves another person and describe the behavior of this person.

3. **Describe the results of the behavior.** What undesirable impact does the behavior have on you? Does it cost you time, money, effort? Does the behavior affect productivity, customer service, quality or morale? It is important to identify how the behavior contributes to a problem so you can explain to the other person why you want him or her to change. These are the logical, rational reasons for changing that allow the other person to consider altering his or her behavior without feeling attacked or judged.

   Example: Terry's behavior creates stress for other family members, which may affect their health; sets an example that younger children may follow; and invites bad feelings rather than an open discussion of alternatives.

   Practice: Using the same problem as in step 2, identify two or three possible results of Rosa's behavior.

_____

_____

FIVE TOOLS FOR SUCCESSFUL CONFRONTATION (continued)

4. **Identify your own feelings.** When the behavior of others creates a problem for you, it is natural to have some feelings about the situation. These emotions will most likely be negative rather than positive, and it is important for you to be aware of them, to acknowledge them and to express them. Denying feelings and holding them in only creates problems. You may do this so much that you experience physical symptoms such as sleeplessness, headaches or worse. When you do finally let out these pent-up feelings, you may do so inappropriately and regret what you say and do.

   Telling someone how you feel actually adds power to your confrontation. Remember the lessons from Part III about how to identify your feelings and how to express them with "I-statements."

   Example: *Concerned* that our family will not enjoy dinner together, *disappointed* and *annoyed* about the late arrivals.

   Practice: Using the same real problem you used in step 2, identify your feelings toward the other person, about the results of the behavior or other aspects of the situation, and write them as "I-statements."

5. **Define the goal you hope to accomplish.** It is not enough to confront someone about his or her behavior; you must get a commitment from the person to change. Without this commitment you have accomplished little beyond getting something "off your chest" (which is okay but not enough to resolve the problem). What do you want? Do you want the other person to stop the behavior in question? Do you want the person to do something else instead of what he or she has been doing? Do you want some ideas from him or her about how to resolve the problem? This last approach is strongly recommended because people are most likely to follow through with a change that was their own idea!

   A final suggestion for this element of the confrontation is to **ask** for what you want. As stated earlier, a command is a little strong for most people in a confrontation situation.

   Example: Will you please give me some suggestions for meals, Terry? Are you willing to be responsible for preparing dinner one evening each week? I would appreciate your help.

Practice: Decide what you want in your problem situation and write your request below.

_____

_____

Taking time to think through the situation and identify these five tools will help you respond more assertively. Responding spontaneously might result in your being nonassertive or aggressive. With practice you can learn to handle such situations spontaneously *and* be successfully assertive. Most people will need to plan and rehearse several confrontations as they learn to think and act in this assertive manner.

When you put all the pieces together, how does an assertive confrontation sound? Remember that this will be a dialogue, not a lecture. You begin the discussion by saying something about the situation, and then the other person responds. What you say next is determined by the person's response and what you plan to accomplish. The better prepared you are, the more flexible you can be when you get unexpected responses from the other person.

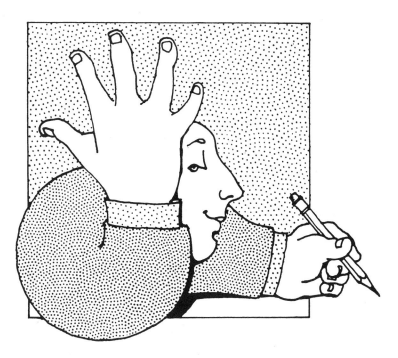

FIVE TOOLS FOR SUCCESSFUL CONFRONTATION (continued)

A Confrontation With Terry

Assuming that Terry is an Expressive teenager, a confrontative dialogue might sound like this:

"Wow, Terry! You really don't like the menu in this joint, huh?"

"That's right! It's boring. We always have the same stuff!"

The parent continues, *"Terry, I'm concerned that your expressing yourself with such disapproving behavior and words will affect our being able to enjoy this time together as a family. If you would like more variety in the meal planning, are you willing to help me by making some suggestions for meals or even being responsible for one meal a week?"*

Terry responds, *"No way! I don't have time for that."*

The parent says, *"Okay. Will you agree not to make such negative remarks at the table in the future?"*

A Confrontation With Rosa

Assuming that Rosa is a Supporting/Caring person, a confrontation might begin this way:

"Rosa, you seemed really flustered in the meeting this morning and uncomfortable with the disruption you caused."

"Oh yes, I was so embarrassed when I spilled my coffee! I knew I was interrupting by coming late again, and I was trying not to call attention to myself, and then I did that stupid thing!"

The manager continues, *"We all have our bad days, Rosa. I was disappointed when you arrived at 8:15 because you promised me you would be on time when you were late last week. What can you do to make sure that you will be present at 8:00 for our future meetings?"*

Do you see how the confrontation is tailored to match the other person's style? Did you notice that not all of the tools were used in each situation? But thinking about all five tools helps prepare you to go in whatever direction the other person seems willing to go. Matching the person's style helps to create a better rapport and increases the probability of getting a cooperative response.

CONFRONTATION DIALOGUE EXERCISE

Use the real problem situation that you have thought through and practice writing what you will say. Guess about how the other person would respond and decide what you would say after that response to continue negotiating for what you want.

Your opening statement: _____

_____

_____

The other's response: _____

_____

_____

Your next statement: _____

_____

_____

The next big step for you will be to actually talk with this person in an effort to resolve the problem. This may take some courage and you may not be completely successful, but you will have taken an important step along the road to becoming more assertive. Even if you do not resolve the problem, you will grow in self-respect and will probably have earned a little respect from the other person as well.

ACTIVE LISTENING

You may be concerned about what to do if the other person responds emotionally and defensively to your confrontation. That is a legitimate concern and a likely occurrence! Probably the most effective technique for handling such responses is empathic listening or Active Listening.*

The idea is to listen carefully when the other person responds to what you have said and prove that you heard and understood by **restating** what you heard. Your restatement needs to be paraphrased so you won't sound like an echo. An effective formula to use is:

▶ **Paraphrase Content.** Summarize the information or thoughts the other person expressed to you. This proves that you understood what he or she said.

▶ **Acknowledge Feelings.** Even though he or she may not have said what he or she is feeling, trust your intuition, make a guess and put his or her feelings into words. This demonstrates your empathy.

▶ **End With A "Check-Out" Question.** Signal that you have finished responding by asking a question such as *"Right?,"* *"Is that what you said?,"* *"Did I hear you correctly?,"* or something similar. He or she will either confirm or correct you, and will feel heard and understood, which helps him or her be less defensive and emotional.

Examples

Terry might react to being confronted about his dinnertime behavior by saying, *"Get real, Mom (or Dad)! All you ever talk about is 'quality time.' We don't have any quality time in this family anymore!"*

What is Terry's unstated emotion? _____

What is the content of the message? _____

_____

What would be your restatement? _____

_____

_____

---

* For a complete treatment of this technique, order *Self-Empowerment* by Sam Lloyd and Tina Berthelot.

Rosa might respond to being confronted about her late arrival by saying, *"I'm sorry. I'm just overwhelmed with everything that's going on in my life right now. I can't seem to get caught up because things keep going wrong, and I'm getting farther and farther behind!"*

What is Rosa feeling? _____

What is the content of the message? _____

_____

What would be your restatement? _____

_____

_____

Author's Answers

Terry seems to be feeling disappointed, hurt, angry, frustrated.

Terry's message was that the family is lacking in quality time together.

An Active Listening response might be: *"Terry, you sound frustrated and disappointed about our not having much time together. Is that right?"*

Rosa seems to be feeling overwhelmed, helpless, frustrated, despondent. The content of her message was that she has experienced a number of problems and she is having difficulty keeping up with her responsibilities.

An Active Listening response might be: *"Rosa, you seem really frustrated about a lot of problems in your life and not being able to keep up with your work. Right?"*

ACTIVE LISTENING (continued)

Even though this may sound simplistic to you as you read about it, the person with whom you are communicating will very likely feel your empathy and understanding and will not even be aware that you have just restated what you heard him or her say. The emotional impact of this type of listening response is powerful and positive, and the result is usually a reduction of stress and defensiveness.

One empathetic response will not result in a person's becoming calm and rational if he or she responded powerfully to your confrontation. You may need to listen and restate several times before the person returns to a normal level of emotion and a willingness to hear you continue your negotiation. *It does work,* but you need to practice a lot to become skillful.

A Case History

A participant in a company training program was taught the technique of restating content and acknowledging feelings, and she was asked to practice with someone before the second day of the program. The young woman decided to practice with her roommate, who was soon to be her husband. She described her experience in class the next morning as an eye-opening experience! When they both were home at the end of their work day, she used her new listening approach without telling him what she was doing. He said, "Boy! I had a really rough day. My boss was on a rampage!" She responded, "Sounds like you're glad this day's over because things were pretty tough at work, huh?"

At this point in her classroom narrative she stopped to explain that her fiancé was a restless type of fellow who would usually walk around when they talked and would sometimes walk into another room during their conversations. She described him as "antsy." When she continued reporting her experience she said, "When I restated what he had said, he just stopped, turned around, pulled up a chair next to where I was sitting and we had a real conversation!" After the training class stopped laughing, she continued by explaining that they talked almost an hour and he remained seated the entire time. She was delighted and amazed that her listening responses had produced such a dramatic result.

It often seems that most of us have the greatest difficulty with communication in our most significant relationships. Few people have any training in managing relationships, and resolving problems in our important relationships can be challenging. But learning how to resolve difficulties in a win-win manner can make a marvelous difference in any relationship. Like everything else in this book, however, it does take practice. We were not taught these techniques and skills when we were young, and none of us will change lifetime patterns of behavior overnight! The following worksheet may assist you with improving your skills in this area. You can use this worksheet for planning and sharing with your significant others, and as a script for your problem-solving discussions.

TALKING OUT PROBLEMS

Set the stage by saying something such as, "I value our relationship and I appreciate your willingness to help resolve problems when they come up."

State the problem. "I am _____ (concerned, angry, etc.) about a

problem and I want your help with it. To me the problem seems to be

_____.

    (As much as possible, avoid using "you-statements" when stating the problem.)

Own your part. "My part in the problem is that I _____

_____.

    (State what you do or do not do, what you assume, how you react, etc.)

Ask for the other side. "How do you see it?" "What do you think about it?" "How do you feel about it?"

Listen and restate.

Make your offer. "To help solve the problem (improve the situation) I am willing to _____.

Ask for what you want. "Will you please _____?

Negotiate agreement on a contract. Summarize what each will give or do.

Set a time for evaluation. Agree upon a date to evaluate how your solution has worked.

Discuss how you have done. If you have done well, have a Celebration! Discuss how you can improve, negotiate a new agreement, express appreciation for each other and renew your commitment to the relationship. If you have not done well, discuss how you can improve or how you might approach the problem differently.

GOALS FOR THE PRESENT AND FUTURE

To avoid taking wrong turns and slipping into former patterns of nonassertive and/or aggressive behavior, practice assertive behavior regularly. First take short trips and then longer journeys.

Short Trips (Short-Term Goals):

► Once a day during the next week spend 10 to 15 minutes at the end of each working day writing assertive statements about situations involving you, or observed by you. Use nonassertive and aggressive incidents and write how they could have been handled assertively.

► Each evening before turning out the light read the "psychological reprogramming" cards you completed on page 23, after achieving a state of relaxation. Do this for three weeks.

► At least once each week for the next three weeks initiate a conversation with someone whose natural style is different than your own. Practice using this style. Notice the positive features of this style and try using them yourself.

Short-Term Goals

By now you probably have some goals you want to accomplish. Write your short-term goals in the spaces below. Remember to make them achievable and positive.

During the next three weeks I will:

1.

2.

3.

GOALS FOR THE PRESENT AND FUTURE (continued)

Longer Journeys (Long-Term Goals):

► Enroll and participate in an Assertiveness Training course or seminar.

► Identify a situation or activity that you have not handled assertively in the past and plan how to handle it assertively in the future. Write out what you will say. Practice delivering it with a friend and then do it!

► Make additional "reprogramming" cards and use them. Review your old cards on a regular basis.

► Read books about assertiveness, personal growth or communication skills within the next month. Cassette tape programs may also be helpful.

Long-Term Goals

Write the long-term goals you want to achieve.

During the next three months I will:

1.

2.

3.

Some of the goals you may want to accomplish might require more than three months. If so, write those goals in the spaces below.

Within the next year **I will:**

1.

2.

3.

GIVE YOURSELF CREDIT FOR SUCCESS

Reliving a special trip through snapshots or movies can be fun and rekindle feelings of pleasure you experienced originally. Following are some suggestions to help you reinforce the success of your new assertiveness skills.

- Tell a friend or family member about a successful assertive experience you had. Ask this person to comment on your success.

- Keep a journal. Write down your assertive successes. The entry does not have to be anything unusual, difficult or dramatic—just so long as it is assertive behavior. Review your journal regularly. Reading about past successes can provide a real "shot" of positive energy whenever you are feeling low.

- Immediately after you have been assertive and are pleased with the outcome, take a few minutes to mentally "record" the experience. Close your eyes and SEE the scene as vividly as possible—FEEL your power, confidence and satisfaction and HEAR your words and voice. While re-experiencing the success with your senses, touch yourself in a pre-determined spot (squeeze a thumbnail, pull an earlobe, etc.) to "set" the experience. In the future, whenever you want to recall the scene and return to assertiveness, touch yourself in the "reminder" spot.

- Reread this book next week and then again in three months. Redo the exercises. Compare the results to your earlier work. Define some new short- and long-term goals. The assertive road to interpersonal effectiveness never ends.

- Share with others. Tell them what you learned about yourself (use I-language!). Share your goals. This will increase your commitment to them. Give copies of this book to others and share with them after they have completed it.

P A R T

Summary and Review

SUMMARY AND REVIEW

Following is a quick review of what has been presented in this book. There are three fundamental behaviors: nonassertive, assertive and aggressive. Of those styles, assertive behavior is the most desirable.

First you took a reading of your own assertiveness. Next you learned to identify each behavior style, and you learned about the basic personality groups: THINKERS, FEELERS and DOERS. These initial insights were provided to help you move toward a "win-win" philosophy of assertiveness.

The 5 Ps of successful change were then presented (protection, potency, permission, practice and proof). Please reread that section to make sure you do what is required to assure your successful development of assertiveness. Remember that self-fulfilling prophecy is a real phenomenon and follow an assertive philosophy. If you expect to be assertive, you will create more success in your life and influence others in a positive way.

Next you learned about the power of psychological programming and were given a way to use it as a tool. You also learned that being assertive requires us to accept responsibility for our thoughts, feelings and behaviors and to use direct, honest, respectful words and accompanying body language.

A refinement of your communication skills was then covered, which encouraged the development of your ability to use all four assertive styles. These styles are Supporting/Caring, Directing/Guiding, Analytical and Expressive. You had an opportunity to identify and practice each style.

After you learned the basics of being assertive and matching assertive styles, you read about several techniques for adding power to your assertiveness. You learned about being patient and repeating, about emphasizing words and phrases, switching from a request to a command, expressing emotions and stating consequences to improve your odds of getting what you want.

The challenge of confronting others was treated with a five-part formula for preparing what you will say to open a negotiation with someone about changing a behavior that you find unacceptable. You practiced identifying each of these important elements as you thought through a real problem situation. A worksheet/script was provided to assist you with talking through a problem with someone.

SUMMARY AND REVIEW (continued)

You were given an opportunity to define some short- and long-term goals, and to practice creating assertive responses for situations. Finally, you were encouraged to continue down the assertive road to interpersonal effectiveness. This book has given you the tools to help you become assertive—it is up to you to apply what you have learned.

Remember, practice will not make you perfect, but it will help you become more assertive. Please read this book again in a week or two, practice your new techniques and skills, and enjoy the rewards of being an assertive person!

NOTES

NOTES

NOTES

NOTES

NOTES

NOTES

NOW AVAILABLE FROM
CRISP PUBLICATIONS

Books • Videos • CD Roms • Computer-Based Training Products

Subject Areas Include:

Management

Human Resources

Communication Skills

Personal Development

Marketing/Sales

Organizational Development

Customer Service/Quality

Computer Skills

Small Business and Entrepreneurship

Adult Literacy and Learning

Life Planning and Retirement

CRISP WORLDWIDE DISTRIBUTION

English language books are distributed worldwide. Major international distributors include:

ASIA/PACIFIC

Australia/New Zealand: In Learning, PO Box 1051, Springwood QLD, Brisbane, Australia 4127   Tel: 61-7-3-841-2286, Facsimile: 61-7-3-841-1580
ATTN: Messrs. Gordon

Singapore: 85, Genting Lane, Guan Hua Warehouse Bldng #05-01, Singapore 349569   Tel: 65-749-3389, Facsimile: 65-749-1129
ATTN: Evelyn Lee

Japan: Phoenix Associates Co., LTD., Mizuho Bldng. 3-F, 2-12-2, Kami Osaki, Shinagawa-Ku, Tokyo 141   Tel: 81-33-443-7231, Facsimile: 81-33-443-7640
ATTN: Mr. Peter Owans

CANADA

Reid Publishing, Ltd., Box 69559-109 Thomas Street, Oakville, Ontario Canada L6J 7R4.   Tel: (905) 842-4428, Facsimile: (905) 842-9327
ATTN: Mr. Stanley Reid

Trade Book Stores: *Raincoast Books,* 8680 Cambie Street, Vancouver, B.C., V6P 6M9   Tel: (604) 323-7100, Facsimile: (604) 323-2600
ATTN: Order Desk

EUROPEAN UNION

England: *Flex Training,* Ltd. 9-15 Hitchin Street, Baldock, Hertfordshire, SG7 6A, England   Tel: 44-1-46-289-6000, Facsimile: 44-1-46-289-2417
ATTN: Mr. David Willetts

INDIA

Multi-Media HRD, Pvt., Ltd., National House, Tulloch Road, Appolo Bunder, Bombay, India 400-039   Tel: 91-22-204-2281, Facsimile: 91-22-283-6478
ATTN: Messrs. Aggarwal

SOUTH AMERICA

Mexico: *Grupo Editorial Iberoamerica,* Nebraska 199, Col. Napoles, 03810 Mexico, D.F.   Tel: 525-523-0994, Facsimile: 525-543-1173
ATTN: Señor Nicholas Grepe

SOUTH AFRICA

Alternative Books, Unit A3 Micro Industrial Park, Hammer Avenue, Stridom Park, Randburg, 2194 South Africa   Tel: 27-11-792-7730, Facsimile: 27-11-792-7787
ATTN: Mr. Vernon de Haas